Harness
The Power of
Celebration

TA-DAH!

Get Happy in 5 Seconds or Less!

Cover design by McPherson Graphics
Interior design by Hixson Media, LLC

ISBN: 978-0-692-29147-4

Printed in the United States of America

First Printing: September 2014

Judy Kay Mausolf
18051 Jay Court
Lakeville, MN 55044
612-701-4922
www.PracticeSolutionsInc.net

"Live a life worth ending with a TA-DAH!"

~ Judy Kay Mausolf

This book is dedicated to
Steve Mausolf, who after over
twenty years together still continues to be
my favorite person in the universe and
my best friend who I can't wait to wake up to
every morning! He makes me smile and laugh
and brings me special coffee!

To my brothers and sisters,
Lorraine, Leatrice, David, Jeanette, Ken & Jim
– just because I love them.

TABLE OF CONTENTS

TABLE OF CONTENTS

FOREWORD

Katherine Eitel

Growing up, altruism was a personal characteristic that was highly valued in my family. Many a bedtime story revolved around a hero who practiced selfless concern for the well-being of others. Over time, without even knowing it, I concluded that putting the pursuit of my own true happiness above all else and all others was the epitome of selfishness. It was a dark moment in my own adult life that would flip that belief on its head.

For decades, I was two people sharing life in one body. There was one version everyone saw as capable, strong, and in control. A selfless mother and wife as well as a remarkable consultant and speaker giving endlessly to her clients and audiences. And then there was the private, mostly hidden version who had denied her own realization of personal happiness for so long and with such pride that she hardly knew what or where it was.

One day, "Version One" was confidently espousing advice to my teenage son on how money did not equal happiness and the indisputable fact that there were countless wealthy and famous people in the world who were miserable and had totally lost touch with what really mattered in life. He interrupted me to ask, "Are you happy, Mom?" Well, of course I'm happy. I'm not talking about me. I'm talking about all those other people. "But you don't seem that happy. Most of the time, you seem either mad or tired or sad." Good grief. What do you all expect? I'm pulled from every direction, trying to keep this family running, the bills paid, and all of you happily doing what you need and want to do. "I know, Mom. I just wish you could have fun and be happy, too, sometimes."

As Judy Kay so memorably promotes, it was one of those out-of-the-mouths-of-babes, "TAH-DAH" kind of moments which echoed and rattled around in my consciousness for days and days afterwards until my internal defenses and well-practiced excuses began to crumble under its haunting reality. It was the truth. I had been living under the illusion that somehow I could give away to others something I did not personally possess; that I could teach a value to my children which I had not learned nor honestly valued for myself. I had put on blinders and earplugs in the form of doing for others and seeing to their happiness and had dutifully ignored the dim, barely audible whisper of my own happiness which was patiently waiting in the recesses of my inner being to flip the light on and allow it to be. In the process, I succeeded in not succeeding. My determination to put their happiness first and leave mine unattended had not made them any happier.

The good news is we are wired for well-being and once I gave it even a little space and attention, it began to blossom and almost effortlessly reveal to me the choices, environments, and paths which would yield the greatest joy and the happiest life. Since that innocent conversation with my son, my life has never been the same and it has become progressively better.

But that's not really the lesson. The best lesson for me has been this: It is the most altruistic way to live in this world to put the happiness of those you love and serve first but you do that best by discovering, practicing, and modeling happiness within yourself.

Judy Kay Mausolf is a shining example of this principle. She just might be one of the most consistently happy people I know as well as one of the most productive and successful clients I have ever had the pleasure of coaching. I first experienced her contagiously positive personality and undeniable courage as a participant in a speaker's training workshop where I was observed her dogged determination to not simply master the art of persuasive speaking but to do it from a platform of authenticity and as a conduit for her own true voice... even if the thought scared her half to death!

Coaches live for those precious moments when you can see latent brilliance in the potential of your students, sometimes long before they can, and you take a chance to push them hard at just the right moment. And then they hate you, right before they love you; Right before the light bulb goes off and shines all over their face with the recognition of their own ability. I'll never forget the way the light shined in Judy Kay's pretty, determined face and I knew that she knew. If you practice the art of coaching long enough, you know when you see genius and you recognize when a student is likely to far surpass the meager talents you have brought to the table. I knew with certainty that Judy Kay had the potential to quickly rise above most of her more experienced counterparts and she has.

TAH-DAH is Judy Kay's second and much anticipated book, in which she brilliantly outlines and showcases her many years of speaking to audiences, consulting with businesses, and coaching teams in the art of working and living from a basis of personal happiness. In this work, Judy Kay not only convinces us of the efficacy of being happy, but she wisely provides us with simple systems and tangible tools to get to it and actually bring it to fruition in a world which does not teach it or provide many examples of how to do it well.

Judy Kay shows us evidence that, to the degree

we can expand our own authentic happiness, we create a stronger platform from which to have more persuasive and influential conversations, positively manage conflict and demands, provide creative alternatives, and recognize collaborative opportunities which are commensurate with that expansion.

Maryanne Williamson said it so well in her famous and oft-quoted passage from A Course In Miracles: "We ask ourselves, 'Who am I to be brilliant, gorgeous, talented, and famous?' Actually, who are you not to be? You are a child of God. Your playing small does not serve the world. There is nothing enlightened about shrinking so that people won't feel insecure around you. We were born to make manifest the glory of God that is within us. It's not just in some of us; it's in all of us. And when we let our own light shine, we unconsciously give other people permission to do the same. As we are liberated from our own fear, our presence automatically liberates others."

Judy Kay Mausolf, in this valuable work, continues this important conversation on the true value of happiness and helps all of us invite many more TAH-DAH moments into our everyday lives.

Katherine Eitel, President, Lioness Learning

Creator of The Lioness Principle

Personal Leadership and Communication Coach

www.LionessLearning.com

Hubby Steve Mausolf and Zoe on a happy ride!

HAPPINESS

Happiness doesn't have anything to do with what we have, where we've been, or who we are. Just look at all the famous and wealthy people who are miserable. Fame, money, stuff or even other people can't make us happy. Happiness comes from within. It comes from what we choose to think about and focus on. Happiness is a choice, and so is unhappiness. We are happy when we choose to be happy. We have a choice: to enjoy our lives or to find fault. We truly do write our own stories of happiness.

"Every moment you make a choice
of what you want to keep, and
what you want to let go of...
and that's how you write your story!"
~ Judy Kay Mausolf

Happiness is not just feel good, nice to have, fluff stuff. When we feel happier more often, we entirely change our beliefs about our world, what we can achieve, and ourselves. Harvard and Mayo Clinic research supports that the happier we are, the more successful, more intelligent, more creative, more productive and healthier we will be.

In every one of us there is this gap between what our lives are like now and what they could be; it is our untapped potential to decide. We can bridge the gap between our potential and our performance by getting happier.

I wrote this book to help people get happier not just for the moment, but for a lifetime. I titled the book "TA-DAH!" because I teach my friends, family, clients and audiences nationwide how to TA-DAH to feel happier in 5 seconds or less. TA-DAH is a philosophy that embodies principles, practices and pearls of wisdom on how to get happier. This book teaches you how to embrace the TA-DAH philosophy and harness the power of celebration.

If you are ready to get happier and be more successful turn the page!

THE ROAD THAT LEADS TO HAPPINESS

Photo donated by sisters, Jeanette & Leatrice Miller

Live Life Big!

We get happier when we stop being afraid to live our lives big. Living life big happens when we challenge ourselves to dream a bigger dream than we could ever imagine…and then take the steps to do it! Life is full of decisions, decisions, decisions… what to do, when, where, why and how! Many of us do not like moving outside our comfort zones. We like to feel safe and secure so we resist making decisions. We don't want to look foolish or fall flat on our faces, and the older we get, the more complacent we become. The problem with complacency is that it drains our passion and happiness. It clips our wings and makes us play ourselves small.

I have heard it said before that "It takes courage to grow up and be who you really are". I think they were talking about how difficult it can be to follow our own authentic path. Others may not agree with our decisions, and some may even go out of their way to dissuade us from even trying. The world is filled with naysayers spewing their opinions of should and shouldn't. If we aren't careful, little by little, others' opinions modify our behavior, and we start to believe that we are who they say we are: smart, not smart; worthy, not worthy; important, not important; good at this or not good at this. We get so worried we won't be accepted, that we cave and start to live our lives a certain way. Pretty soon, we live a life of should: what others think we should be, the way they think we should look, the way they think we should act. We pretend to be a certain way in order to be accepted and avoid rejection.

"Don't let the fear of
what others might think
determine your actions!"
~ Judy Kay Mausolf

Little children haven't had their wings clipped with should and shouldn't. They dance and twirl and sing out loud just because they feel like it. They wear things that make them happy even if it may not seem appropriate to an adult. There is never a wrong time to wear a super hero cape and mask or princess dress with glass slippers. What's wrong with being a super hero or princess every day? Children don't worry about or let what others might think stop them. They are free to live by how they feel in the present moment.

Niece - Amelia Mausolf

"Live your life your way;

let others live their lives their way!"

~ Judy Kay Mausolf

We are unique and our uniqueness is our gift to the world. Why would we ever want to be led astray with other people's shoulds and shouldn'ts and follow in someone else's footsteps?

It is necessary for each of us to chart our own path regardless of our fear of the judgment or rejection. It is how we will discover our purpose and happiness that leads us to our greatest potential. Unless we try to do something beyond what we have already mastered, we will never become what we might have become.

"Plant the seed in your mind,
care for it,
work steadily toward your goal,
and it will become reality."
~ Unknown

What do you think about on a day-to-day basis? We are the sum total of our own thoughts. The stories we tell ourselves become the life we live. If we believe we can't... we can't! Luckily, the same holds true that if we believe we can... we can! We are where we are because of what we think. What we think today, tomorrow, next month, next year determines our future. Our doubts, fears and worries can stop us from attempting.

Photo donated by sisters, Leatrice & Jeanette

"Your life is a reflection
of what you believe it can be!"
~ Judy Kay Mausolf

When we have faith in ourselves, we follow our gut instincts that we are born with. We become more powerful when we trust ourselves. Decisions about what we like or don't like or what we want or don't want become very clear when we trust our gut instinct. Our happiness soars when we align with what is authentic to us to live our life big.

Action Plan – Live Life Big!

Here is an action plan I read about and have used for years to get happier by living life big.

- Draw a large circle in the center of the page. Inside the large circle draw a medium circle and inside the medium circle draw a small circle. It should look like a bulls-eye when you are finished.

- Think about what is important to you. What makes you happy and feeds your passion? Imagine inside of the large circle all the possibilities for enriching your life: all your talents developed, your passion, your curiosities satisfied. Write them down inside the large circle and label the circle Possibilities.

- Next, think about all the things you have thought about trying but haven't - a new hobby, a new class, or even just a new way to organize your tasks. Write them down inside the medium circle and label it Want to Try.

- Now think of all that you have actually experienced so far in your life, all that you can do, and all that you know you enjoy. Write them inside the small circle and label it My Life Now. Your drawing should look like a bulls-eye with the outer circle labeled Possibilities, the middle circle labeled Want to Try, and the center circle labeled My Life Now.

- Look at the space outside of the circle titled Possibilities. That's where you want to be - out there seeking experiences you haven't even considered that could enrich your life! That's where the juice is! That's where you will find fulfillment, happiness and your greatest success!

"What Ifs"

We get happier when we are able to overcome our fears. Overcoming our fears empowers us to worry less and feel more confident, which result in making us feel happier. The fear I am talking about is the fear of "what if". It can stop us from walking our own paths and living a life of possibilities. You know; What if I make poor choices? What if I am headed in the wrong direction? Or worse yet, what if I fail?

We make excuses for why we can't or won't do something. When the truth is that it is our fear of "what if " that stops us. The more we dwell on it, the bigger it seems. We can spin ourselves into a frenzy. We have all done it at one time or another.

Our fear of "what if" is what keeps us small! We all have different "what if" fears. They start at a very early age. If you were like me, you were afraid of "What if there was a boogeyman under the bed?". I can remember jumping from the doorway onto the bed and clearing the floor to avoid having him get me! Luckily, the bedroom I shared with my sister Jeanette was very small.

Me with my three sisters.
Left to right – Leatrice, Jeanette, Lorraine & Me.

The fear of "what if" continues to live on in our lives and doesn't just limit itself to the boogeyman under the bed. It manifests itself into new fears. Fear of failure, fear of not being good enough, fear of not being liked or accepted, fear of judgment or criticism, fear of retaliation, fear of not being able to handle the situation; in essence, simply the fear of "what if".

"What others think of you
has very little to do
with who you really are!"
~ Judy Kay Mausolf

How many times have you changed your mind about doing something because of saying to yourself, "But what if this happens"? You just "what if'd" yourself right out of action. Think about this. It's a biggy! How many times has fear stopped you? The ironic part is that fear is really only a negative prediction of the future. In most cases, what we worry about doesn't happen. What actually happened, we didn't even think about or worry about, and yet we still survived. It's proof that worry is a total waste of energy and time. If we can learn to evaluate the real danger, as opposed to the perception of danger (what if), we will get a more realistic viewpoint and we will be less afraid to act. Whether or not we act is based on our confidence in being able to handle the situation. Instead of worrying, think about an action plan. Having a clear plan will empower you with the confidence needed to take action.

Imagine how much happier you would be right this second if the fear of "what if" had no impact on your decisions. What would you do or try? What would your life look like right now?

Action Plan – "What Ifs"

Here are action questions to help you stop the fear of "what if" from stopping you. I suggest writing your answers down to make your plan of action more concrete.

- What is the worst case scenario?

- What is the best case scenario?

- What is the most likely thing to happen?

- What is my specific plan if the worst thing happens?

- What is my specific plan if the best thing happens?

- What is my specific plan if the most likely thing happens?

- Will I live? If the answer is yes...proceed!

Joy in the Journey

We get happier when we take time to enjoy the journey and not just the end result. What does the path look like to your personal happiness and success? Is it a spouse, a family, good health, new career, weight loss, riches or maybe all of the above? Whatever it is, do you take time to smell the roses along the way? Are you enjoying the detours in the road or are you focused only on traveling a straight path?

"When you celebrate only the end result,

you lose the joy in the journey!"

~ Judy Kay Mausolf

Easy Living rose in my garden

Do you ever say to yourself,

"Once I achieve _____, then I will _____."?

We often delay allowing ourselves to feel good about our accomplishments until we reach our ultimate goal. You may have a goal to lose thirty pounds and you have only lost twenty. Instead of feeling good about our accomplishment of losing twenty pounds, you focus on the ten pounds you haven't lost. Oftentimes, once we reach our goal we feel empty because we have not learned how to enjoy the present success. It became all about achieving the goal and not about finding joy in the moment. If your only thought once you achieve your goal is "Now, what's next?", you lost your joy along the way.

Steve with niece Rylee!

In order to feel happy once we achieve our goals, we must first learn to find joy in who we are and where we are and see the beauty in the present moment.

Action Plan – Joy in the Journey

Here are the action steps to help you find joy in the journey, even when things don't seem like they are going your way.

- Get present. Close your eyes and breathe in through your nose and out through your mouth deeply, five times for a count of five. It will help you reset to think more clearly, problem solve and stop spinning out of control.

- Tell yourself, "This is where I am supposed to be right now."

- Next, ask yourself, "What am I supposed to learn from where I am right now to help me understand the next step I am meant to take?"

- What do you see, hear, touch, smell and taste in the moment that brings you joy?

- Take the time to explore, experience and enjoy the moment and you will find joy in the journey.

Who knows? It may be the bend in the road you didn't want to take that leads you to your greatest happiness and success!

LIFE STANDARDS
THAT LEAD TO HAPPINESS

Wake Up Your Awesome

We get happier when we are proud of who we have become. It happens by waking up our awesome; in other words, becoming our best us. What would waking up your awesome be when it comes to attitude, communication, and performance? What are your core life standards you want to live by in your personal and professional life? In essence, what is your code of conduct?

"There was a time when you were five years old, and you woke up full of awesome. You knew you were awesome. You loved yourself. You thought you were beautiful, even with missing teeth and messy hair and mismatched socks inside your grubby sneakers. You loved your body, and the things it could do. You thought you were strong. You knew you were smart. Do you still have it? The awesome."

~ Unknown

Some people set standards that are just good enough to get by while others are only happy with perfection. The dictionary describes good enough as "passable, tolerable, and unexceptional", and perfection as "supremacy, exactness and faultlessness". What if we change our thinking from being good enough to being awesome enough, and leave perfection totally out of the picture? Think of awesome enough as doing your best to be inspiring, excellent and first-rate!

Awesome is not about being perfect. It is about doing your best in the current circumstances. Some days we will do better than others. We will make mistakes and that's okay as long we learn from them.

Mistakes are what help us to grow. Humans are the only animals on earth who punish themselves and others over and over for the same mistakes. We are not here to sacrifice our joy in life to become perfect.

Set awesome life standards to live by even when it is difficult or you don't feel like it.

CHAPTER 1

Action Plan –
Wake Up & Be Awesome

If you can't answer yes to each of these questions, you may have some room to become even more awesome.

- Am I happy with how I live my life, who I am and what I do?

- Do I impact others in a positive manner?

- Do I strive to do my best?

- Do I offer the highest quality of care, service or skills that I can based on the current circumstances?

Eared Grebe - Photo donated by sisters,
Jeanette & Leatrice Miller

Model the Waddle

We get happier when our relationships are built on trust and respect. If you want others to trust and respect you, "model the waddle!" In other words, live your standards in action, not just words. It is next to impossible to build trust and respect if you do not. How can anyone trust and respect someone who says one thing, but does another? We don't support or follow people we don't trust and respect. People will do as you do, not as you say. Actions always speak louder than words. If you say one thing and do another, people will start to doubt and be suspicious of everything you tell them.

They may lose trust that you're doing the right thing, or that you even know what you're doing, and will stop following your lead. The vision you're trying to make happen will falter if people don't trust and respect you.

"When you lead by example

you create a picture of what's possible!"

~ Judy Kay Mausolf

Think about the people in your life that you trust and respect the most. Why do you trust and respect them? It is because we can rely on them. They consistently do what they say, when they say, and how they say they will do it. Trust and respect do not just happen overnight. They take time to nurture and grow. However, breaking one's trust and respect can happen in a heartbeat. We can maintain trust and respect when we model the waddle and live a life founded on awesome life standards.

Action Plan – LIFE STANDARDS:

- Establish life standards to wake up your awesome.

- Create a list and label it "My Awesome Life Standards".

- Sample List

    o I will use my words to lift instead of tear down.

    o I will go directly to the source and resolve the issue.

    o I will help others when I see that they need help.

    o I will ask instead of assuming.

    o I will finish what I say I am going to do.

    o I will focus on the greater good instead of WIIFM (What's in it for me).

- o I will tell the truth, and be kind, caring and compassionate.

- o I will not take things personally.

- o I won't gossip about others.

- o I won't be late or absent for trivial reasons.

- o I will do my best based on the circumstances.

- Print it, frame it and put it on display for future reference.

- Model the waddle – even when you don't feel like it.

- Live and maintain your standards regardless of circumstances.

CHAPTER 3

RELATIONSHIPS THAT LEAD TO HAPPINESS

Lift Others

We get happier when we lift each other up to shine! When we focus on helping others, we feel good. When we feel good, we are happier. Not one of us has gotten to where we are today on our own. We've all received help from someone who inspired, encouraged, taught us, opened doors, trusted and supported us. It is because of that mentorship that we are where we are today.

I would like you to take a moment and think about who lifted you up in life. Who was there for you to help you up when you had fallen? Who opened doors when they were all closed - sometimes even locked? Who believed in you enough to help you believe you could take the first step in reaching your dreams? Wherever you are right now, take a moment to give thanks!

"We are all here to

lift each other up to shine!"

~ Judy Kay Mausolf

Now, think about who you believe in that you can lift up by opening doors to help them succeed. Who do you know in your personal and or professional life that could use a little lift? What can you do to help them tune out the noise and turn up the volume to the lighter, brighter side of life?

Action Plan – Lift Others

- Choose five core people you want to inspire, challenge and love.

- Ask them how you can most help them. What doors do they need opened?

- Offer them suggestions – why re-invent the wheel?

- Introduce them to others who will support their happiness and success.

- Make time to communicate, connect and collaborate with them often.

Link With Lifters

We get happier when we surround ourselves with relationships that lift us up. Surround yourself with people who love, respect and believe in you, people who will support you with both their words and actions. Don't waste your precious time on those who don't. Life is too short! If every time you are around someone they consistently discourage, tear you down or make you feel less than awesome, maybe it's time to let go of that relationship.

Two very happy people!

Character Traits of Lifters:

- Communicate kindly, honestly and respectfully

- Are reliable

- Ask and don't assume

- Sometimes disagree and don't take things personally

- Resolve conflict quickly

- Have fun and laugh often

- Share success secrets

- Share goals and dreams

- Are accepting of differences

- Are willing to forgive and apologize

- Love freely

"Surround yourself with people you love,
who love you!" ~ Judy Kay Mausolf

Eileen & Jerry Millard – Awesome example of love
(Our friends for over 20 years)

Love is the greatest lifter of all. There is nothing more powerful than love! When we feel loved, we feel happy and empowered to do things even outside of our comfort zone. Knowing I have my husband Steve by my side cheering, supporting and loving me has given me the confidence to live an even bigger and juicier life than I could have ever imagined.

Whenever I am coaching clients or speaking to an audience, I focus on coming from a place of love. This is about them, not about me. I want them to feel hope and learn skill sets that will help them be happier and more successful. I want people to feel good about themselves because they have been with me.

Love in action produces happiness and empowerment and can change our world.

Action Plan – Link with Lifters

- Evaluate your relationships with the traits of Lifters.

- Surround yourself with people who love, challenge and inspire you to live your dreams.

- Choose your core people.

- Make time to communicate, connect and collaborate with them often.

- Eliminate the relationships that consistently discourage, tear you down, or make you feel less than awesome.

CHAPTER 4

STRATEGIES THAT
LEAD TO HAPPINESS

Ask For What You Want

We get happier when we are not afraid ask for what we want in life. Just ask! It sounds so easy, so why don't we just ask? I don't know about you, but I was taught at a very early age that it was impolite to ask for things. I now realize that philosophy was ridiculous. People can't read our minds. How could they possibly know what we want or need? It leaves everything up to assumptions - and we all know what assumptions make - they generate an emotional reaction cycle. That is what you were going to say right? We believe it is not proper to ask for what we want in life. We believe that if people love us, they should know us well enough to know what we desire or how we are feeling.

*"If you don't ask for what you want
don't be angry when you don't get it!"
~ Judy Kay Mausolf*

Even really good relationships are sometimes destroyed because of these false beliefs. We make assumptions that everyone sees life the way we do; that they think, act and respond the same way we do. Therefore, we believe their actions mean the same as if we did the same actions. They must like and want the same things we want, so they should know what we like and want. Ask for what you want to avoid assumptions!

Action Steps –
Ask For What You Want

- Think about the results you want to achieve.

- Go directly to the source(s).

- Clearly explain what you want to achieve and why it is important to you.

- Ask and be specific about what you want.

Ask Instead of Assume

We get happier when we stop making assumptions. Something happens and we instantly assign meaning to it. That is an assumption.

We start imagining what other people are doing, what they're thinking, what they're saying about us. We invent an entire story based on assumptions, and we believe it. One assumption leads to another assumption; we jump to conclusions and we take things personally. Most conflicts are based on false assumptions. Assumptions are nothing more than false stories that we tell ourselves.

This creates a big drama for nothing because we don't know if it is really true. It may be correct or it may be incorrect. We won't know unless we take the next step. ASK. Do you see a recurring theme?

When you get that twinge in your gut and you think, "Hmmm - I wonder what they meant by that, or I wonder why they haven't...?", or you find yourself saying "I think they meant this" - you don't know! Stop yourself immediately from wondering and speculating and ASK. You will be much happier with a lot less drama and false assumptions.

Action Steps – Ask Instead of Assume

Ask with care, concern and respect, and never with judgment or criticism.

- I am not quite sure what you meant, please tell me more?

- I am not quite sure what happened. Can we talk about it?

- Is everything okay?

- Are you okay?

Act "As If"

We get happier when we feel more confident. You may have heard the saying, "Act as if." It is a common catchphrase that means to imitate confidence so that as the confidence produces success, and it will generate real confidence. The purpose is to avoid getting stuck in a self-fulfilling prophecy related to one's fear of not being confident. Walk, talk and carry yourself exactly as you would if you were completely confident in a particular situation. It is the Law of Reversibility in action.

The Law of Reversibility states, "If you feel a certain way, you will act in a manner consistent with that feeling. Likewise, if you act in a manner consistent with that feeling, even if you don't feel it, you will create a feeling that is consistent with your actions." In other words, how we act is how we begin to feel. The brain executes the same neural pathways in the same way, whether you're viewing real life situations or imagining them. The mind cannot tell the difference between the real world and an imaginary world. This is one of the greatest breakthroughs in gaining confidence.

Acting "as if" empowers us to do the things that will make us happier and more successful. There is never a better time than the current moment to go after what you want in life. So what do you want to do different with the rest of your life? What will make you happier? I often hear, "I am too old to change or to start over now". Really? Regardless of how little time it may seem you have left, it is the rest of your life. Is there really ever a time when it is too late to be happy for the rest of your life?

Muir Woods

"The best time to plant a tree

was always twenty years ago.

The second best time

is always today."

~ Unknown

I have heard life has three stages. The first stage is from birth to 29 years of age. Of course, we all know that these are the years we are the smartest!

The second stage is from 30 to 59. These are the building, producing, and creating years. We often find ourselves in the midst of raising our families, building our careers, and scrambling to make ends meet. This is the stage when it is easiest to lose focus on what is important and what makes us happy in life. Often, we take a back seat to everything else and lose ourselves in the process.

When we lose ourselves; happiness, success and sometimes even our relationships go out the window.

The third stage is life after 60. This stage is when it finally becomes about us living an authentic life that makes us happy. We stop caring so much about what other people think, and instead focus on how we feel. Many bucket lists are started in this stage. Our mortality becomes real and we want to make up for lost time. Life becomes about finding peace and wellbeing and living in our happy place.

"Live your dreams now
to any degree that you can!"
~ Judy Kay Mausolf

My mom, Ione Miller, shared this pearl of wisdom; "Don't wait until you are old and have enough money to do some fun things. You may never make it to old age. If you do happen to stay alive, they are not nearly as much fun or as important to you as they would have been when you were younger." Mom and Dad would have so loved to have gone on a cruise in their earlier years instead of waiting until they were in her late sixties. It would have been a much needed break from the hard work of raising seven kids on a farm. The joy and fun my parents would have experienced would have by far outweighed the cost and would have meant the world to them. My mom was a very smart lady who left us way too soon.

Childhood Farm, St. Anthony, ND

I challenge this three stage process thinking. Why wait until we are sixty years old and two thirds of our lives (or more) has passed to start being in our happy places? Most of us know someone who worked hard all their life and waited until retirement to live their dreams... only to pass away before they could even start. Why not find ways to align with our purpose and passion and be happy in every stage of our lives?

Action Plan - Act "As If"

- In every stage, take time to evaluate your life.

- What brings you joy and happiness?

- What would you like to see different?

- Identify limiting beliefs that hold you back.

- Live your dream in any capacity you can.

- Act "as if" and take the first step.

- Don't give up the first time something doesn't work.

R.I.S.E.

We get happier when we can successfully implement and sustain changes that help us succeed. The R.I.S.E. is a concept of best practices to help people form habits that will empower them to implement and sustain change. A way for people think differently, act differently, make healthy decisions and achieve their goals. R.I.S.E. is an acronym for Review, Implement, Sustain, and Evaluate.

Hot Air Balloon Ride/Napa Valley

"Every day is a new opportunity

to do it even better!"

~ Judy Kay Mausolf

Action Plan – R.I.S.E.

- Review - Review what you are currently doing, and what's in it for you in your personal and professional life if you change!

- Introduce/Implement - Clearly define the action, process, system, standard or protocol. Clarify what, who, when, where, why and how to establish as SOPs (Standard Operating Procedures).

- Sustain - This is the most important step! Be precise, consistent & realistic with routines & repetitions. Ask yourself if it is realistic to accomplish with the time allowed, equipment available and current training you have. If not, address the obstacles and roadblocks. Consistency is a must if you want to implement and sustain the change successfully (five out of five times). Continue repeating the same process until it becomes so automatic it becomes a habit. Whenever we implement something new, there is a learning curve and it may feel awkward or uncomfortable. The average transition period it takes to learn something new to when it becomes a habit is 66 days. Precise and consistent repetition helps to shorten the transition period.

- Evaluate - Schedule quarterly check-ins with yourself to evaluate what is working and what is not in your life to continue to self-diagnose.

CHAPTER 5

GET HAPPY

Tulips that choose to be O.R.A.N.G.E.!

O.R.A.N.G.E. Power

We get happier when are surrounded with the color orange. My husband Steve, teases me about living in an orange bubble. Those of you who know me know that the color orange plays a big part in my life and my business brand.

So what is O.R.A.N.G.E. power? Different colors generate different energy and emotions. The color orange creates feelings of happiness and positive energy! I surround myself with orange to inspire happiness and positive energy. I am mindful of the energy I am radiating out. A happy and positive attitude is one of my core values that defines how I choose to live my life.

You may have heard our attitude determines our altitude in life. Our attitude affects our altitude by creating positive or negative energy in the environment around us. The energy we create can generate either our success or our failure, based on the Law of Attraction.

My ORANGE Gerber Daisies!

"Everything affecting you
is a reflection of the energy
that you are radiating."
~ Judy Kay Mausolf

I am an acronym addict and wanted one for O.R.A.N.G.E! My husband Steve and I came up with it on a seven hour drive to visit my family home in North Dakota. So are you ready? O.R.A.N.G.E. stands for Optimistic Radiant Attitudes Nurture Great Energy! O.R.A.N.G.E. is simply about radiating a positive attitude to create great energy in our lives. In other words, if you radiate an optimistic attitude, you will nurture great energy in your environment. It's the Law of Attraction in action!

"Life is a gift.

Our attitude determines how we live it!"

~ Judy Kay Mausolf

The Law of Attraction is like seeks like based on the frequency of energy emitted. All energy has different vibration frequencies. Positive energy seeks other positive energy with the same frequency, and negative energy seeks other negative energy with the same frequency. The energy we radiate out there always resonates back to us. We do create our environment whether it is positive or negative!

Action Plan – O.R.A.N.G.E. Power

- Surround yourself with what makes you feel happy and positive – like the color ORANGE.

- Be mindful of the energy you are radiating.

- Choose to radiate positive energy.

Choice Power

We get happier when we choose to be happier. Have you ever thought, "I was in great mood until "_____" happened"? When we allow "_____" (whatever the blank is at the moment) to affect how we feel, we are in essence relinquishing our power and allowing circumstances to control our emotions.

If we allow our circumstances to control our emotions, we become a victim of our circumstances.

The truth is that circumstances don't dictate how we feel - we do! It is always our choice!

Hubby Steve's happy place - fly-fishing on the river!

"To get up each morning
with the resolve to be happy
is to set our own conditions
to the events of each day.
To do this is to condition circumstances
instead of being conditioned by them."
~ Ralph Waldo Emerson

I am often asked how I stay so happy and positive. I will share with you that it is not only because I meet nice people. I meet some of the same people that you meet who are not always so lovely! It's also not because my life is perfect or that everything is easy. I have had many difficult times and things don't necessarily go my way. Instead, it is a choice I make when I wake up every day! It's a choice to be happy and positive regardless of what may come my way. I choose to smile and impact others in a positive manner regardless of their behavior. I choose to not relinquish my power to circumstances or allow them dictate whether I am happy or not.

"Happiness is always
our choice!"
~ Judy Kay Mausolf

I created two unique orange rubber bracelet bands to wear as a visual reminder that we always have the choice to be positive, happy and celebrate life! One reads "Smile & Shine" and the other reads "TA-DAH!" They are the first thing I put on every day. It may seem silly, but they make me feel like I have super powers. They empower me to smile and celebrate life regardless of the circumstances!

You can find them on my website at www.PracticeSolutionsInc.net under the resources/products tab.

Action Plan ~ Choice Power

- Wake up.

- Put on your power band.

- Affirm it is going to be an awesome day.

- Choose to be positive regardless of how you feel.

- Choose words and actions that have a positive impact.

Smile Power

We get happier and make others happier when we smile. Smile energy is extremely powerful and wide spreading. A smile instantly creates positive energy in the environment and uplifts the mindsets of the giver, the receiver, and everyone in the vicinity. People want to spend time around people that make them feel better. Smiles are contagious.

*"Smile big at everyone
you meet today and see if
your world doesn't seem
a whole lot friendlier."
~ Judy Kay Mausolf*

Smiles everywhere!

A simple smile can change how you and
everyone around you feels. Try to think of
something negative and keep smiling. It is

very difficult to do. When you smile, your body recognizes it as a positive body pattern and sends a message to you that everything is okay, and that life is great. Smiling changes our mood. When you're feeling sad, or stressed, start smiling and you will feel instantly better.

Smile when you don't feel well to improve your health. A smile can boost your immune system by improving your general feelings of well-being. Smiling makes you feel more relaxed which reduces your blood pressure and feelings of stress. People who smile live an average of seven years longer than people who do not. So get happier and live longer by smiling often every day!

Action Plan – Smile Power

- Make eye contact.

- Smile genuinely.

- Don't worry about their response and whether they smile back or not. It's not important.

Laughter Power

We get happier when we laugh more often. Add a regular dose of laughter to every day and you will not only be happier, you will also be healthier! However, it is not always so easy to do. We get so busy that we focus only on getting the job done. We don't slow down enough to take time to laugh. We need to add laughter to our list of daily priorities!

Whenever I am not traveling, I get to wake up in my own bed with hubby Steve and our dog, Zoe. She is the funniest little dog who makes us laugh every day! We actually get up an hour earlier each day just to spend time with her. Zoe's day starts with a trip outdoors for a little fresh air, and then it's back into bed for some tummy rubs. Next, it's time for hair and teeth brushing (healthy white teeth are important in the Mausolf household), followed by a little breakfast and ending with playtime with her favorite toys: Fetch, Sandwich and Snaggles!

Zoe!

"You don't stop laughing
because you grow old.
You grow old because
you stop laughing."
~ Michael Pritchard

Laughter triggers healthy physical changes in the body. A good, hearty laugh:

- Relieves physical tension and stress, leaving your muscles relaxed for up to an additional 45 minutes

- Boosts the immune system

- Decreases stress hormones

- Increases immune cells and infection-fighting antibodies, improving your resistance to disease

- Triggers the release of endorphins, the body's natural feel-good chemicals. Endorphins promote an overall sense of well-being and can even temporarily relieve pain

- Improves the function of blood vessels and increases blood flow, which can protect you against a heart attack and other cardiovascular problems

Now that I have your attention, it's time to practice laughing! That's right; it's just like anything else. If you want to be good at it, you have to practice. Start chanting out loud ha ha, ho ho, ha ha, ho ho, ha ha, ho ho, ha ha, ho ho, ha ha, ho ho, ha ha ha ha ha ha ha ha ha ha…okay I know you feel silly…keep going and continue chanting until you laugh heartily.

Think about it. When was the last time you had a hearty laugh? No, I am not talking about a little chuckle. I am talking about a throw your head back, side holding, tears streaming, almost wet your pants laugh! You don't need to have a sense of humor, be happy or have any reason to laugh. Just laugh for the sake of laughing!

Action Plan – Laughter Power

- Fake it until you feel it.

- Continue repeating ha ha, ho ho until you laugh heartily at yourself.

- Schedule time to practice laughing every day.

- Surround yourself with people and things that make you laugh.

The more you practice laughing, the better you will become and the happier you will feel!

S.P.F. Power

We get happier when we change our focus to positive. You can be happy even when life seems difficult. Here is the big secret about staying happy and positive in difficult times. It does not take any super powers or anything special, although a TA-DAH or Smile & Shine Band can give a burst of positive super power. It is simply a clear understanding of the power of focus.

"Our focus creates our attitude."

~ Judy Kay Mausolf

The myth about attitude is that we are born with either an attitude of a cup half full or half empty. The reality is that our attitude is a learned behavior. Having a positive attitude is a skill. If you focus on the positive, you will have a positive attitude. If you focus on the negative, you will have a negative attitude. When you hear people say they are in a bad mood, it is because they choose to linger in the negative emotions. The physical part of any emotion only lasts thirty seconds or less. Any emotion after thirty seconds comes from hanging on to the emotion. Woe is me people, or what I refer to as wallowers, choose to be victims of their emotions. They wallow in them like a mud bath and tell everyone how miserable they are in hopes of eliciting sympathy. They actually enjoy the drama and negative emotions.

The science behind the thirty seconds of emotion pertains to fight or flight. Our immediate responses to negative or positive emotional stimuli are the result of a chemical reaction in our brains. Responses such as a rush of adrenaline, lump in our throats, being out of breath, a dry mouth, sweat running down our backs, faces turning red, nervous laughter, flailing and kicking, and tears welling up in our eyes - these responses happen in the first five seconds. In the next 25 seconds, we battle to take control of our bodies. It is best not to suppress nor deny the emotion, but to let ourselves feel it, observe the physical effect on us, mentally step aside from it, and let it go.

After thirty seconds, we are past the fight or flight stage and the prefrontal cortex (cognitive portion of the brain) kicks back in, which allows us to think logically again. Nearly all intended behavior, including attitude, is learned and so depends on the cognitive part of our brain. Our prefrontal cortex allows us to access and implement what we need to produce any attitude or behavior we choose.

We can choose not to be negative, angry, hurt, stressed, frustrated, grumpy or whatever. It is always our choice. Instead, focus on finding a reason to be happy and feel good in every situation.

Action Plan - S.P.F. Power:

Here are action steps to achieve S.P.F. Power:

- Whenever you feel stressed and in the fight or flight zone, breathe deeply and count to ten, slowly for thirty seconds.

- Feel and observe the physical reaction and then let it go.

- Identify three positives in the situation. Even in the most horrific circumstances there are positives.

- I also like to always keep three positives in my hip pocket just in case I am struggling to see the positive in the present moment. My three positives are my husband Steve, my health, my dog, Zoe, my family, my career. (OK, I couldn't limit it to three.) When I think about my positives, I instantly feel grateful and happier.

- Ask yourself "How can I not be happy when I am so blessed?"

- Shift your focus from what is negative, missing or bad to what is positive, present and good.

Labeling Power

We get happier when we use neutral or positive words instead of negative words to label. Words that label have tremendous impact on our attitudes and happiness. It is important to be mindful how we label the relationships, events and outcomes we have in life. If we label something as bad, it becomes our belief and we manifest feelings to match. I find using the word "interesting" instead of "bad" eliminates the negative power.

Photo donated by my sisters, Jeanette & Leatrice Miller

Label the day as awesome
and you set yourself up to succeed!"
~ Judy Kay Mausolf

Our beliefs of positive and negative are based on our past experiences. If we do something and we have what we believe to be a negative outcome, we will label it as negative. Yet we may have an entirely different outcome if we attempt to do it again. For example, I went on a hot air balloon ride over Napa Valley for my fiftieth birthday (just a few short years ago). It was serene and wonderful. I am even afraid of heights and I would do it again in a heartbeat. I would label it as a very positive experience. However, the following day, the winds came up unexpectedly and the balloons had a difficult time landing and one was blown into a power line. I would have labeled it as negative had I gone that day... and most likely would never consider going again. The good news is we can change our belief from negative to positive when we continue to add new positive experiences.

Truthfully, how can we label something as good or bad if we don't know what happens in the end? None of us have a crystal ball. So how do we really know if something is good or bad? There have been many things in my life that at the time seemed... interesting, that actually turned out generating a very positive outcome. Haven't we all thought or said "This is going to be bad" at one time or another, and yet it turned out to be one the best things to happen to us?

Action Plan – Labeling Power

- Label things as interesting instead of bad or negative.

- Don't let one bad experience stop you from trying again.

- Consider the positive possibilities.

- Create an action plan to succeed.

- Worst case scenario, chalk it up and label it as a learning experience.

Mindful Talk Power

We get happier when we are mindful of our self-talk. The majority of self-talk takes place so quickly and automatically that we don't even notice we are doing it. Even if you don't really listen to your chatter, your subconscious mind is listening. The subconscious mind just accepts everything you tell it, and responds accordingly.

"Words and thoughts have their own energy, including self-talk."

Everything you think and say
affects the way you feel."
~ Judy Kay Mausolf

Some examples of negative self-talk are:

- Worry - Fear of "what if"

- Perfectionism - Not good enough or should haves

- Self-Criticism - Comparing yourself to others, with you being the loser

- Self-Doubt - Lack of confidence that you can do or achieve your dreams

- Being a Victim - You have no control over your circumstances, life happens to you, and you have bad luck.

The awesome news is we can hard wire our brains to start thinking more positively! When we have mindful talk, actively choose where to focus our thoughts, and repeatedly apply it to a wholesome and constructive thought, we eliminate the negative deceptive self-talk.

Positive affirmations are like planting seeds in the ground. It takes time to go from a seed to a mature plant. It takes consistency and time from the first declaration to the final demonstration. You can't just say something positive once and expect it to appear. Today's affirmations drive our future happiness and success!

When I am about ready to present I think of how I want to be with my audience. I practice words like connecting, loving, authentic and present.

Action Plan – Mindful Talk Power

- The minute you start to judge, criticize or compare and think about yourself as anything less than awesome, stop and change the verbiage in your head.

- Define how you want to feel or be today. Choose words or a phrase to describe that feeling or state of being. It could be words like happy, successful, healthy or awesome. If you can, stand in front of a mirror and make eye contact with yourself. Okay, I know this seems a little weird, but it's a good weird! It is important to say it out loud as if it already exists. "I am... ". It must be I am, not I want. It is more powerful when you say it out loud and your mind believes it already exists because you stated, "I am". For example, I am happy, I am awesome, I am going to make positive things happen today, I am going to make good decisions today, I am going to rock it today, I am going to have an awesome day! You can say as many things as you want. There is no limit to positive self-talk!

- Say it with passion, conviction and attitude! Think about the level of happiness and success you want to attract. The more energy and emotion you put into it, the more you attract! It's the Law of Attraction in action.

- Replay the same message over and over throughout your day. Ask yourself; do my words and actions support those feelings or state of being? Reset if necessary to align your words, actions and state of being.

- End your day by saying out loud how you felt or your state of being for the day. I was happy today. I was awesome today! I made others smile today. I helped someone today! I made a difference today! I changed someone's life today!

- Get over how it may look to others! We are so afraid someone may see us saying positive affirmations and we will look silly or weird. So what if someone hears us? We are all a little weird.

Celebration Power

We get happier when we celebrate life every day. There is a power in celebration. Celebration lifts our spirits and empowers us to instantly feel happier. Celebrate even the little things everyday regardless of how simple, normal or mundane it may seem.

North Dakota Crocus - photo donated by sisters,
Jeanette & Leatrice Miller

See the value even in the little things in life. Celebration is really just a way of publicly showing thanks and praise. Practice privately and publicly celebrating what is already in your life instead of focusing on what is missing.

"Everything is here until it's not…

celebrate every second!"

~ Judy Kay Mausolf

Celebration not only makes us happier, it reduces our stress level, which makes us smarter. When we are stressed, our prefrontal cortex shuts down. That's the cognitive part of our brain that helps us process, create, problem solve and think and behave rationally. It's the smart part of our brain. We can feel happier, reduce our level of stress and get smarter in less than five seconds, AND we have the ability to make it happen whenever we choose. It may sound too good to be true. However, it is scientifically proven to work.

If we change our physiology (body patterns) when we are stressed and feeling unhappy, we can change our psychology (how we feel). Body patterns are the repeated actions our body reflects when we feel certain emotions. They are how our body speaks to us and therefore, have a direct connection to our moods. Some examples of negative body patterns that make us feel stressed are rubbing temples, wringing our hands, frowning or a hunched over, closed position. Our body recognizes these patterns as a call from us to send stress hormones. The more stress body patterns we do, the more stress hormones are released and the worse we feel. It is a perpetuating cycle of negativity.

Whereas smiling, laughing, or a victory pose are positive body patterns that will help us feel happier. A victory pose is holding your arms air in the shape of a "V". For example when runners run a across a finish line they throw their hands up in the air to celebrate their victory. These are all signals to our bodies to send serotonin, the happy endorphins, which make us instantly feel happier, less stressed, smarter and give us a sense of wellbeing. So, if we are feeling stressed and want to change our moods to be happier, all we have to do is change our body pattern!

I teach TA-DAH as a way to change our physiology to change our psychology in less than 5 seconds. I started doing TA-DAH when I was a small child. Maybe you did too. Do you remember when you were a little kid and you would do something you thought was pretty cool in front of people? For example a somersault or a little dance and you wanted to celebrate your success. Did you ever throw your arms up in the air and shout "TA-DAH!"? It was a victory pose.

Our bodies recognize TA-DAH as a positive body pattern and instantly send the happy endorphins that reduce our stress, make us smarter, happier and healthier, which all lead to greater success!

The awesome part is we can recreate that feeling of happiness and wellbeing whenever we want. All by just shouting a passionate TA-DAH with a smile and a victory pose. Now, if you only said the word TA-DAH in a less than enthusiastic tone and did not smile or do the victory pose, you would not feel any differently.

My Hinman audience celebrating with a TA-DAH!

So let's take a moment and practice doing a TA-DAH together! Tija and Tom, are you ready to help lead? On the count of three, I want you to smile, throw your arms into the air and shout in your loudest voice... "TA-DAH!"

Should we do it once more? Why not?
Now seriously... how do you feel?

Action Plan – Celebration Power

- See the value in even the normal, simple or mundane things in life.

- Celebrate each accomplishment in your day regardless of how small.

- Celebrate even when you don't feel like it – it will lift you up.

- Do a TA-DAH at least once a day. There is no limit to how many you can do.

Leave Happy

I would like to leave you by sharing pearls of wisdom from my dad, Clem Miller. He lived a very happy life and left us in 2009. I so miss our daily phone calls where we solved all the world's problems. He said, "The worst failure in life is having regrets at the end for what you didn't do! It is important to be happy in life and to do it; you figure out what's important to you and make time for it. You do the best you can with what you know. You continue to learn and grow to make sure you know. You make it your day every day. At the end of the day, if you can look back on the day and know you gave it your best shot... .well, that's pretty much as good as it gets."

Action Plan – Leave Happy

- Make time for the things and people that matter.

- Continue to learn and grow.

- Make every day your day.

- Give it your best shot every day.

My dad, Clem Miller
He would have wanted me to say he was out standing in his field!

"Perhaps they are not stars in the sky.
But rather openings where
our loved ones shine down
to let us know they are happy."
~ Unknown

So come on and get happy!

TA-DAH!

ABOUT THE AUTHOR

Judy Kay Mausolf is the owner and president of Practice Solutions Inc. She is a speaker, coach and author with expertise in communication and team relationships. She teaches dentists, managers and their team how to grow their practice by becoming better leaders, communicating and working together better and delivering service with more passion and fun. She travels nationally and internationally, speaking at workshops, study club groups, specialty practice seminars, and conventions as well as coaching individuals and business owners to succeed.

She is Past President of National Speakers Association (Minnesota Chapter), Director of Sponsoring Partners for the Speaking and Consulting Network, and a member of the National Speakers Association and Academy of Dental Management Consultants. She is author of *Rise & Shine* and a contributing author for many dental magazines. She is also author and publisher of the monthly newsletter "*Show Your Shine*".

Judy Kay lives a happy life residing in Lakeville, Minnesota, with her favorite person in all the universe, her husband, Steve Mausolf, and Zoe, their exuberantly happy seven pound Yorkie!

NOTES